Beautiful
Beaded Rings

D&C
David and Charles

ACKNOWLEDGMENTS
Thanks to Tout à Loisirs for supplying the colour chart and the equipment used in this book.

Chief Editor: Meriem Varone
Editing: Hélène Pouchot, with Sandrine Andrews
Proofreading: Madeleine Biaujeaud
Layout and illustrations: P.A.C. studio@pakenko.com
Photography: Cactus Studio – Fabrice Besse
Stylist: Sonia Roy
Technical Co-ordinator: Anne Raynaud
Photoengraving: Arts Graphiques du Centre

The designs in this book were created by:
VÉRONIQUE NARCY (PP14–17; 30–31; 34–37; 46–47; 52–55);
MARIELLE ELOY (PP12–13; 22–26; 28–29; 32–33; 42–45; 48–49; 56–57; 60–63);
DOMINIQUE MABILEAU (PP10–11; 20–21; 38–39; 58–59);
ISABELLE DELHAYE (PP18–19; 26–27; 40–41; 50–51).

A DAVID & CHARLES BOOK
Copyright © Dessain et Tolra / Larousse 2004

David & Charles is an F+W Publications Inc. company
4700 East Galbraith Road Cincinnati, OH 45236

First published in the UK in 2006
Originally published as *Irrésistibles bagues de perles* by Dessain et Tolra,
France 2004

English translation Copyright © David & Charles 2006

A catalogue record for this book is available from the British Library.

ISBN-13: 978-0-7153-2293-2 paperback
ISBN-10: 0-7153-2293-1 paperback

Printed in China by SNP Leefung
for David & Charles
Brunel House   Newton Abbot   Devon

Visit our website at www.davidandcharles.co.uk

David & Charles books are available from all good bookshops; alternatively you
can contact our Orderline on 0870 9908222 or write to us at FREEPOST EX2 110,
D&C Direct, Newton Abbot, TQ12 4ZZ (no stamp required UK only); US customers
call 800-289-0963 and Canadian customers call 800-840-5220.

Contents

Key to symbols

★

Easy

★★

Intermediate

★★★

Advanced

A WEALTH OF GLITTERING RINGS
FOUR DESIGNERS, FOUR UNIQUE STYLES

*With their shimmering beads and radiant colours,
these beautiful and inventive rings are the work of four designers.*

Véronique Narcy selects her colours with the precision of a mosaic artist. She uses brightly coloured rocaille beads to make her jewellery and her flowers are as beautiful and fresh as the real thing!

The costume jewellery of **Dominique Mabileau** rivals any made from precious stones. In her simple designs, light and reflection are the key to creating spectacular, radiant pieces.

Marielle Eloy is passionate about crystal beads and loves to incorporate them into her graceful and inventive designs. Carefully calculated shapes and tones make her rings as sophisticated as antique jewellery.

Isabelle Delhaye reinterprets classic jewellery on a larger scale. She likes to fuse styles and recycle beads. Her jewellery is dazzling and exuberant: the stuff of the Arabian Nights.

BASIC EQUIPMENT

Always read through the projects carefully before starting to ensure you have all the necessary equipment and materials to hand. Store your beads by size and colour so that when you come to choose those you need for a design, it will be easy to see whether you have the required amounts.

WIRES AND THREADS

Wires and nylon threads provide the basic structure for the rings and carry the beads. The choice of wire or thread will affect the overall look of the ring and how well structured it is.

Nylon threads come in a variety of colours and thicknesses. Use these strong, flexible and subtle threads to make rings with an invisible structure that fit your fingers snugly. When using nylon thread with bicone beads, try not to rub the thread against the beads when tightening, as this may cause it to snap.

Brass wire (gold-plated, silver-plated and black) and silver wire are more prone to snapping than nylon thread but are nevertheless good to work with and will give your rings a more solid structure. To save on costs, you could substitute silver-plated brass wire for silver wire.

TOOLS

Wire-cutters
Use wire-cutters to cut wire of all thicknesses. Standard scissors are suitable for cutting nylon thread.

Flat-nosed pliers
These pliers are used by electricians. Choose a pair with a very fine tip to grip your thread or wire when working.

Round-nosed pliers
Use these pliers to make small hoops in the wire used with the paste beads to fix them on to your rings.

MOUNTS AND FINDINGS

Eyepins
These small lengths of metal wire are used to make small hoops for use with some types of bead.

Ring mounts
They consist of two parts, a ring and a perforated base plate, into which you thread your nylon. They are made in gold and silver and come in round and oval versions.

BEADS

Rocaille beads

These small beads are made in glass, metal and crystal and may be clear or opaque. They come in over 350 colours. Most rocaille beads are round, but they can be other shapes, too.

If you intend to create a piece made entirely out of rocaille beads, why not use beads in the same colour from different sources?

As colour dyes are never the same, even slight differences in tone can result in a more vivid and iridescent ring that will catch the light better. Thread on your beads at random.

Bicones

Bicones look like small spinning tops and are the queens of beaded rings. They are used to make centre motifs rather than the band, because their shape makes them uncomfortable to wear against the skin.

Bicones come in plastic, glass and crystal versions. Perhaps the most well-known types of bicone are Swarovski crystals, made by the company established by Daniel Swarovski in the 19th century. In 1892 Swarovski manufactured the first precision crystal-cutting machine.

Bicones generally come in 5mm, 6mm and 8mm sizes. The large-scale ring designs are made using 8mm bicones.

Faceted beads

Faceted beads come in a wide range of sizes and colours. You can buy them in crystal, glass and plastic versions. Their facets create interesting effects as they reflect the light. Depending on their size, you can use them to make the central motif or the ring itself. They have a more oval shape than rocaille beads.

Round beads

These beads come in crystal, glass and plastic and their surface may be smooth or faceted to catch the light. Depending on their size, they too may be used to make the centre motif or the ring itself.

Teardrop beads

As their name suggests, these beads have a teardrop shape. They come in faceted and smooth versions. Teardrop beads are made in crystal, glass and plastic.

Spacer beads (rondelles)

These small beads are narrow and concave. They are often made of metal and can be threaded on as spacers between round or faceted beads.

Use spacer beads as a means to gracefully bring out the centre motif of your ring. Some are inlaid with crystal paste or jet, others come in antique silver or gold.

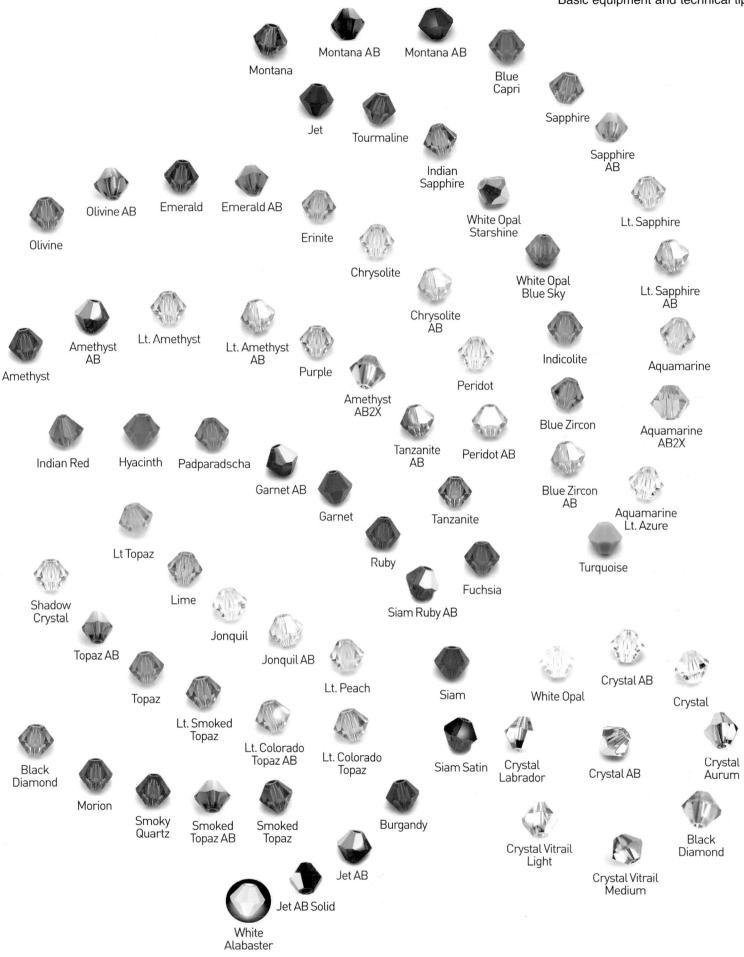

Montana

Montana AB

Montana AB

Blue Capri

Jet

Tourmaline

Sapphire

Sapphire AB

Indian Sapphire

Olivine AB

Emerald

Emerald AB

White Opal Starshine

Lt. Sapphire

Olivine

Erinite

Chrysolite

White Opal Blue Sky

Lt. Sapphire AB

Chrysolite AB

Amethyst AB

Lt. Amethyst

Lt. Amethyst AB

Purple

Peridot

Indicolite

Aquamarine

Amethyst

Amethyst AB2X

Tanzanite AB

Peridot AB

Blue Zircon

Aquamarine AB2X

Indian Red

Hyacinth

Padparadscha

Garnet AB

Garnet

Tanzanite

Blue Zircon AB

Aquamarine Lt. Azure

Lt Topaz

Ruby

Fuchsia

Turquoise

Shadow Crystal

Lime

Jonquil

Siam Ruby AB

Topaz AB

Jonquil AB

Topaz

Lt. Smoked Topaz

Lt. Peach

Siam

White Opal

Crystal AB

Crystal

Lt. Colorado Topaz AB

Lt. Colorado Topaz

Siam Satin

Crystal Labrador

Crystal AB

Crystal Aurum

Black Diamond

Morion

Smoky Quartz

Smoked Topaz AB

Smoked Topaz

Burgandy

Crystal Vitrail Light

Black Diamond

Jet AB

Crystal Vitrail Medium

Jet AB Solid

White Alabaster

AB = aurora borealis

TIPS AND ADVICE

Use the diagrams in this book to help you make up your rings.
We have added text to complement the diagrams only where further explanation is necessary.
Weaving rings is first and foremost a visual exercise. Making rings has never been so simple with our
easy-to-follow step-by-step diagrams showing bead types and colours, threads and wires.

Véronique Narcy's rings are made up of several pieces which are then put together and require several wires, so we have added text to help you when making up her designs. The designs of Dominique Mabileau, Marielle Eloy and Isabelle Delhaye use a single wire or thread and are less complex to reproduce. Their rings are made up by following the step-by-step diagrams.

Starting off

Regardless of whether you are working on a design that uses nylon thread or wire, you should always start by threading the first few beads into the centre of your wire or thread.
The black arrow on the diagram indicates the starting point.

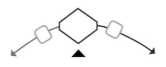

Following the diagrams

White beads indicate beads that are coming into play for the first time. Grey beads are those that are already in place. This will give you a sense of how your ring is taking shape.

Crossing threads and wires through beads

In every diagram you will see that the wires or threads are crossed inside beads. This is a very common technique for weaving beaded rings: you will master it very quickly and will need it in all your designs. This method is widely used to make up the ring itself, but not exclusively.

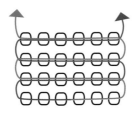

Making a ring

Generally, the band which goes round the finger, from each side of the decorative upper design, is made using small rocaille, faceted or round beads. We have not always shown all the beads you will use in the band in our diagrams because the length of the band will depend on the girth of your finger. You are likely to need 6 to 10 3mm faceted beads and 24 to 40 rocaille beads. Simply cross the wires or threads to make a thin strip of beads, as shown in the diagram.

Finishing off

Wire:

When you have finished weaving your ring, cross the two wires through the first row, then through the next few rows. Trim the excess wire close to a bead and thread it back into the bead so that it does not stick out. The green and red dotted arrows in the diagrams indicate where you should join your wires. To trim black and silver-plated brass wire twist it back on itself. It will snap right beside the bead.

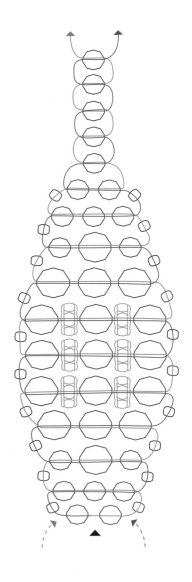

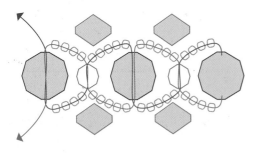

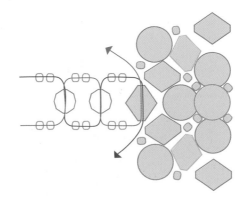

Nylon thread:
Once your ring is made, secure the two ends of thread to the other side of the ring base. Thread the nylon back through the first row of beads to secure, ending with both ends together in a row. Tie a knot and hide it between your beads. You can apply a little glue to the knot.

If you have the patience to do so, thread your nylon back through several rows to secure it before finishing off.

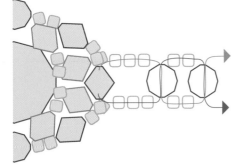

Repairs and reinforcements
There is no easy way to repair a nylon or wire ring. If your ring falls apart or snaps, you will have to redo it. It is possible to reinforce rings made from brass wire by creating a border in black wire. To do this, take a length of black brass wire, start at the centre of a row, thread it through your beads and come out at one side. Next, weave a border around your ring as shown in the diagram. When you have finished one side of the ring, do the same on the other side.

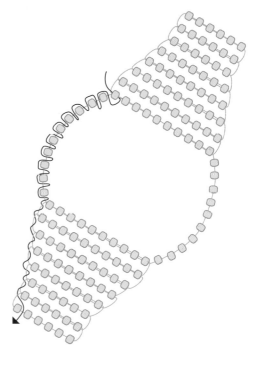

DESIGNING YOUR OWN RINGS

Once you have made some of the pieces in this book, you will probably be inspired and want to create your own rings.

Before starting on your own designs, here are some helpful tips and advice:

Drawing up a pattern
If you have not purchased your beads yet, start by drawing up a pattern for your design. Use the diagrams in this book as a guide and for inspiration.

This will give you a better idea of what size, shape and colour beads you will need. Feel free to use coloured pens or pencils to help you. This will prevent unfortunate mistakes such as buying too many expensive beads, choosing incompatible colours, or creating poorly proportioned designs.

Choosing colours
Use the reference chart of over 70 colours given on page 7 to help design your pieces and decide on your choice of beads before you purchase them. The names on the chart apply to other beads, too.

Before buying them, put a few beads in the palm of your hand to get a better idea of how your colours will blend or clash. Opt for brash, bold colours or more subtle tones to suit your taste and style. To bring out a particular colour, combine it with a large number of beads in another colour that will highlight your first colour.

Making up other shapes
You can achieve a dome-shaped ring not only by the size of beads you use but also by tightening your ring base wires or threads to a lesser or greater extent, as in the Tortoise ring. A square or rectangular shape is dictated either by the shape of the centre bead (as in Butterfly and Odalisque) or by the choice of design. By repeating the square base shown in the Square design you will obtain a larger squared ring, and repeating the motif six times over will give you a large rectangle.

SIMPLE RINGS*

Simple to make and beautifully elegant,
these stunning rings play on light and transparency.

MATERIALS REQUIRED: **SIMPLE RING**

- 32 shadow crystal faceted beads, 4mm
- 32 shadow crystal faceted beads, 3mm
- 32 silver rocaille beads, 2.5mm
- 32 jet on silver paste spacer beads, 4mm
- About 80cm (32in) brass wire, 0.25mm

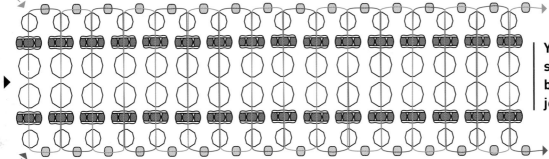

> You could substitute simple metal spacer beads for the expensive jet paste spacers.

MATERIALS REQUIRED: **DOMED RING**

- 12 crystal aurora borealis faceted beads, 6mm
- 24 crystal labrador faceted beads, 4mm
- 48 matt silver rocaille beads, 2.5mm
- 24 antique silver spacer beads, 6mm
- About 80cm (32in) brass wire, 0.25mm

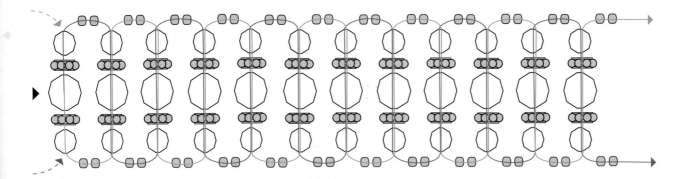

PRINCESS★★

*Classic lines combine with citrus colours
in this very fashionable design.*

MATERIALS REQUIRED

1 large round faceted bead, 10mm

14 crystal bicones, 4mm

8 to 12 small round faceted beads, 4mm

1 tube rocaille beads

About 80cm (32in) nylon thread, 0.25mm

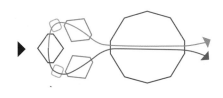

1

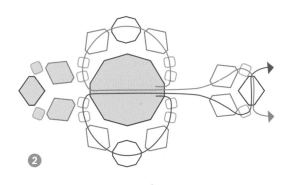

2

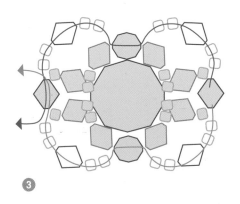

3

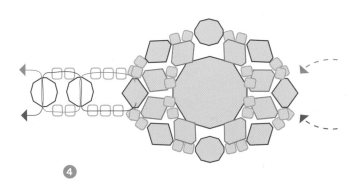

4

DOME ★★★

*This dome ring is simply divine. Tighten the central beads
to create a stunning cone-shaped ring.*

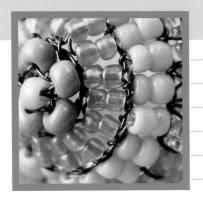

MATERIALS REQUIRED

- ○ **5 grey rocaille beads, 2.5mm**
- ○ **About 90 translucent violet rocaille beads, 1mm**
- ○ **About 90 translucent grey rocaille beads, 1mm**
- ○ **41 turquoise rocaille beads, 2.5mm**
- **About 80cm (32in) silver-plated brass wire, 0.25mm**
- **About 1.50m (59in) black brass wire, 0.25mm**

The dome

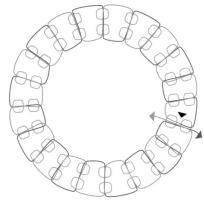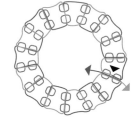

Motif 1

① Using the diagram as a guide, make up a circle comprising 20 rows of turquoise rocaille beads with a 20cm (8in) length of black brass wire.

Motif 2

② Make up a second circle, this time slightly convex, comprising 15 rows of violet rocaille beads threaded on to a 20cm (8in) length of black brass wire.

Flower

③ To make up the centre of the dome, make a slightly convex flower with 5 petals using the 2.5mm grey rocaille beads and a 10cm (4in) length of black brass wire. Trim the outside end of wire, then thread a turquoise rocaille bead on to the inner wire. Next, thread your wire between the wires in the beads on opposite sides of the circle. Go back through the centre bead, then trim close to the edge of your work.

④ To assemble the three motifs, take a 20cm (8in) length of black brass wire. Thread the wire into a row in motif 1, leaving a short length. Lay motif 2 in the centre of motif 1 and attach as shown in the diagram. Lastly, place the flower in the centre of motif 2, and attach following the same method as before.

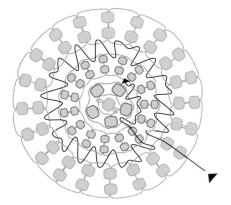

The band

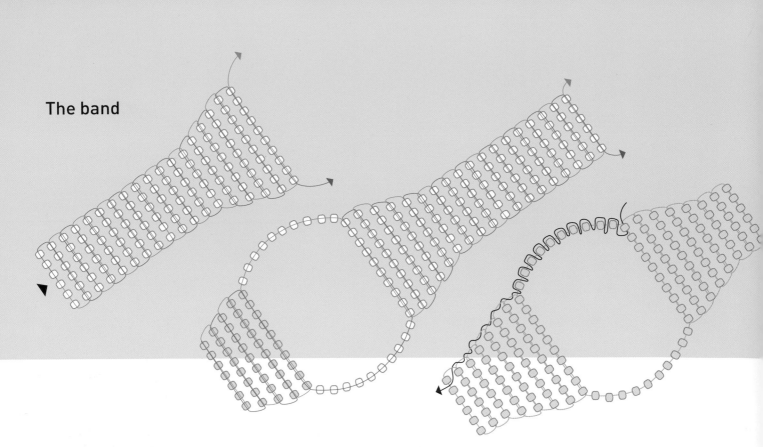

① To make up the band, use an 80cm (32in) length of silver-plated brass wire and translucent grey and violet rocaille beads and position them as shown in the diagram.

② To make the circular section, thread 10 rocaille beads on to each end of wire. Next, thread 10 more beads on to one of the lengths of wire and pass the other end of wire through these 10 beads. Then make up the second half of the band as shown in the diagram.

③ To finish off the band, make a border using a 40cm (16in) length of black brass wire, weaving it along the band, around the row of 10 beads at the centre of the ring, and continuing to the end of the band. Repeat on the other side of the ring.

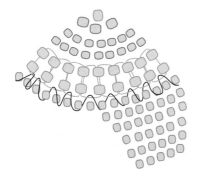

④ Lastly, mount the dome on to your ring using a 30cm (12in) length of black brass wire.

This pointed dome was made using rocaille beads comprising 7 soft green peridot beads, 14 purple beads and 42 plum-coloured beads and about 150 opaque and translucent violet beads for the band. To achieve the conical effect, make your circular motifs more convex.

MATERIALS REQUIRED

○ **55 grey rocaille beads, 3mm**

▫ **53 translucent mauve rocaille beads, 2mm**

⬡ **1 translucent blue round faceted bead, 4mm**

About 1m (40in) silver-plated brass wire, 0.25mm

About 1.50m (59in) black brass wire, 0.25mm

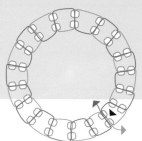

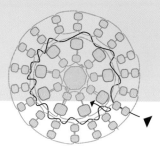

Motif 1

❶ Make up a circle motif with 9 rows of grey and mauve rocaille beads using a 15cm (6in) length of black brass wire. Trim the outside end of wire, then thread a translucent blue faceted bead on to the inner wire. Next, thread your wire between the wires in the beads on opposite sides of your 9-row circle. Go back through the centre bead, then trim.

Motif 2

❷ Make up a second circle motif with 22 rows using mauve rocaille beads and a 70cm (28in) length of black brass wire.

❸ To put the two motifs together, with motif 1 in the centre of motif 2, thread a 20cm (8in) length of black brass wire into one of the rows in motif 1, leaving a short length. Weave the wire between motifs as shown in the diagram.

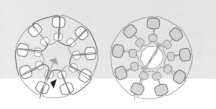

❹ Using a 50cm (20in) length of silver-plated brass wire, make up two bands from grey rocaille beads, each with between 20 and 25 rows depending on the size of your finger. Next, make borders on both with black wire.

❺ Join the two bands using a 15cm (6in) length of black wire, leaving the centre 12 beads out of your weaving. Join the two ends of your band together. Space out the 12 central beads on the band to make a circle.

❻ Place the central motif in the circle and attach it to the ring with a 15cm (6in) length of black wire. To put the finishing touches to your ring, thread the wire around the central motif in the same way that you would make a border.

SCHEHERAZADE★★

An exuberant ring fit for a sultana. The showy colours at the centre are tempered by the use of more subtle beads on the band.

MATERIALS REQUIRED

9 round glass, crystal or mother-of-pearl beads, 6mm

12 crystal bicones, 6mm

10 round faceted beads, 4mm

1 tube rocaille beads

About 80cm (32in) nylon thread, 0.25mm

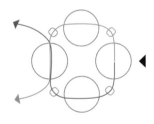

①

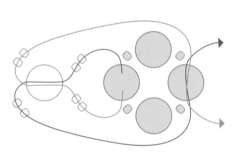

②

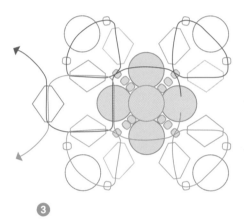

③

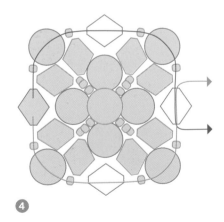

④

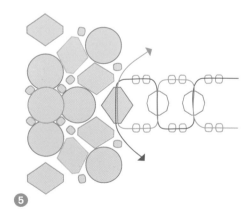

⑤

This ring was made using silver rocaille beads, purple crystal bicones and a round silver bead, giving it a cooler tonal colouration.

ECHO *

In this stunning ring there's no need for coloured beads:
your crystal beads will reflect the changing colours around them.

MATERIALS REQUIRED

19 crystal labrador faceted beads, 4mm

17 crystal labrador faceted beads, 6mm

20 crystal rocaille beads with metal hole, 2.5mm

6 crystal paste on gold spacer beads, 6mm

About 80cm (32in) brass wire, 0.25mm

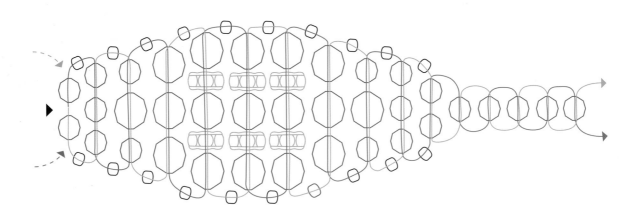

To make the blue and black ring, use jet AB crystal faceted beads,
black rocaille beads and crystal on grey paste spacers.

LACE ★★★

Whatever colour combination you choose to make this model,
the end result will be a very fine ring that will sit delicately on your finger.

MATERIALS REQUIRED

46 crystal bicones, 3mm

1 tube mini rocaille beads

6 to 10 round faceted beads, 3mm

About 1.50m (59in) nylon thread, 0.25mm

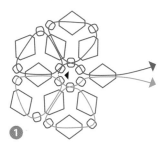

①

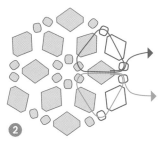

②

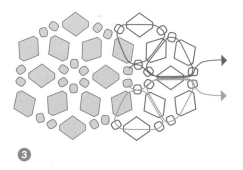

③

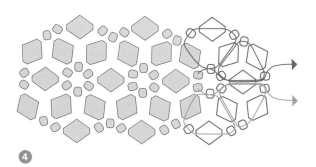

④

5 Position your threads either side of the base in a symmetrical fashion to make up extra flowers. Thread the nylon into the side beads as follows: 1 bicone, 2 rocaille beads, 1 bicone; thread on 1 rocaille bead, 1 bicone, 1 rocaille bead, 1 bicone and 1 rocaille bead, then go back into the same bicone and 1 rocaille bead to make a loop.

Next, thread on 1 rocaille bead, 1 bicone, 1 rocaille bead, 1 bicone and 1 rocaille bead and go into 1 bicone in the previous loop and 1 rocaille bead in the second loop. Continue in this way, using the diagram above as a guide.

6 To reinforce and finish off your centre motif, thread 1 rocaille bead, 1 bicone, 1 rocaille bead, 1 bicone and 1 rocaille bead on to your nylon and thread it back into your work, following the outline of the motif as indicated in the diagram. Repeat with your other thread. Make up the band to fit your finger using rocaille and faceted beads as shown in the diagram.

Why not accentuate the flower motif using white crystal bicones interspersed with blue crystal bicones?

VARIATION: TORTOISE***

MATERIALS REQUIRED

40 crystal bicones or faceted beads, 4mm

1 tube rocaille beads

6 to 10 faceted beads, 4mm

About 1.50m (59in) nylon thread, 0.25mm

To make the Tortoise, follow steps 1, 2, 3 and 4 for the Lace ring. When you have made up the three flowers in the centre motif, proceed as follows.

⑤ Arrange your threads on either side of the base in a symmetrical fashion to make the side flowers. Thread the nylon into the side beads as follows: 1 bicone, 2 rocaille beads, 1 bicone; thread on 1 rocaille bead, 1 bicone, 1 rocaille bead, 1 bicone and 1 rocaille bead, then go back into the base bicone and 1 rocaille bead to make a loop. Thread on 1 rocaille bead, go into the second base bicone and thread on 1 rocaille bead, 1 bicone and 1 rocaille bead and attach to the bicone on the previous flower.

Go back into 1 rocaille bead, 1 bicone and 1 rocaille bead, then thread on 1 rocaille bead. Go back through the third base bicone and lastly thread on 1 rocaille bead, 1 bicone and 1 rocaille bead to finish the centre motif.

⑥ To make a neat outline, tighten your ring and shape it with your fingers. Thread the nylon around the motif on either side as shown in the diagram and add your final bicones. Finally, bring the threads towards the centre bicones in the motif to start the band.

ODALISQUE★★

Make this delightfully feminine ring your own by placing an oval or round bead at the centre to make a rectangular or square motif.

MATERIALS REQUIRED

4 crystal bicones, 8mm

20 faceted beads, 4mm

1 round or oval central bead, 12mm

1 tube rocaille beads

About 80cm (32in) nylon thread, 0.25mm

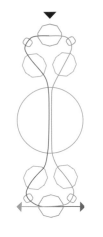

❶

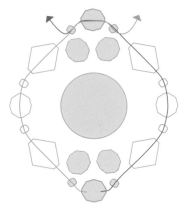

❷

❸ Thread on 8 to 12 rocaille beads depending on the size and shape of the centre bead.

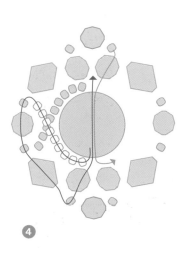

❹

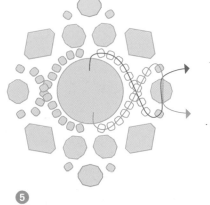

❺

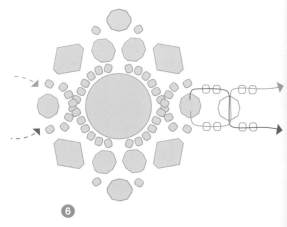

❻

CRUSADER ★★

A timeless and precious-looking ring with a touch of the medieval.
Why not experiment with other colours?

MATERIALS REQUIRED

⬡	3 round faceted beads, 8mm
⬡	About 18 round faceted beads, 4mm
◇	6 large crystal bicones, 6mm
◇	4 small crystal bicones, 3mm
○	1 tube rocaille beads
	About 1.50m (59in) nylon thread, 0.25mm

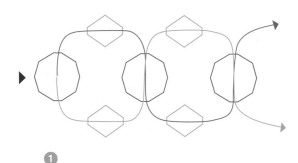

①

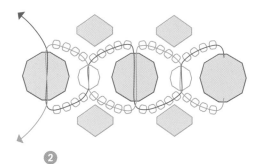

②

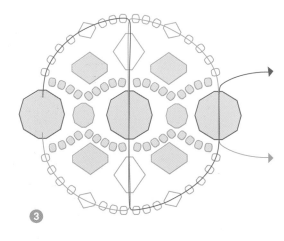

③

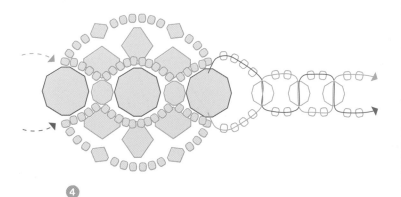

④

STRIPES*

*This multicoloured striped ring echoes the work of a mosaic artist;
or you could opt for a more subtle monochrome approach.*

MATERIALS REQUIRED

- 100 turquoise rocaille beads, 2mm
- 25 violet rocaille beads, 2mm
- 25 peridot rocaille beads, 2mm
- About 2.50m (98in) silver-plated brass wire, 0.25mm
- About 2m (79in) black brass wire, 0.25mm

▶

1. Use a 50cm (20in) length of silver-plated brass wire to make up two rings in violet rocaille beads, each with 20 to 25 rows (depending on the size of your finger).

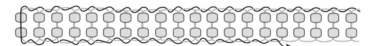

2. Make a border on each ring with black brass wire.

3. Next, make up three rings of 20 to 25 rows using a 50cm (20in) length of silver-plated wire: the first in peridot, the second turquoise and the third violet, then make a border around each of them with black brass wire.

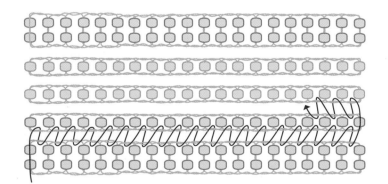

4. Join the five rings with a 50cm (20in) length of black brass wire as shown in the diagram.

THISTLE ★★★

The geometrical nature of this ring makes it suitable for use with a variety of colours and motifs. The ring works equally well with contrasting colours or complementary tones.

MATERIALS REQUIRED

⬡	38 to 42 faceted beads, 4mm
◇◇◇	48 crystal bicones, 4mm
○	1 tube rocaille beads
	About 1.50m (59in) nylon thread, 0.25mm

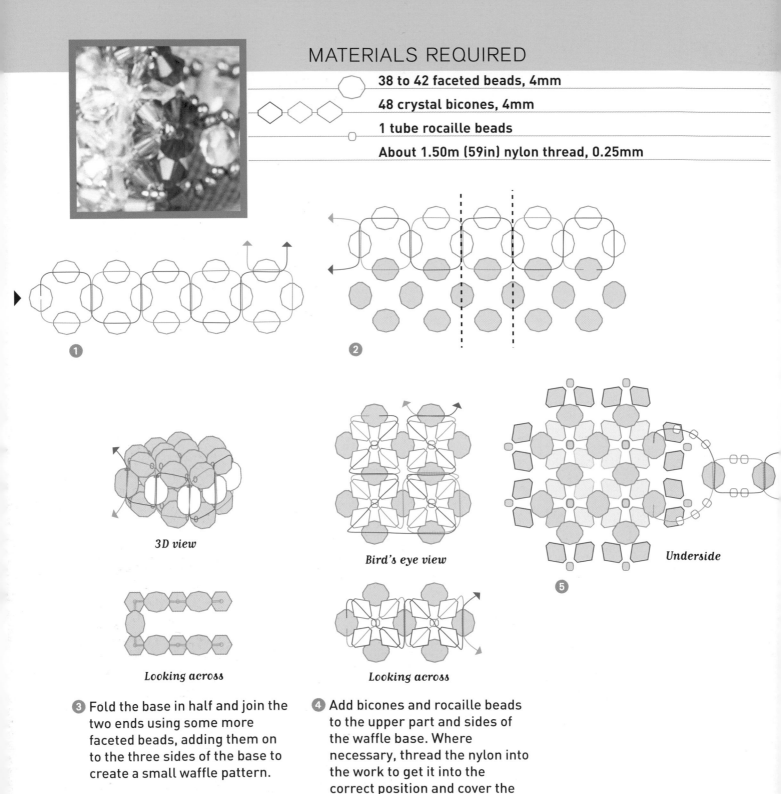

3D view

Bird's eye view

Underside

Looking across

Looking across

❸ Fold the base in half and join the two ends using some more faceted beads, adding them on to the three sides of the base to create a small waffle pattern.

❹ Add bicones and rocaille beads to the upper part and sides of the waffle base. Where necessary, thread the nylon into the work to get it into the correct position and cover the five sides.

BOUQUET ★★★

Graceful rings set with bouquets of sparkling crystalline beads.

MATERIALS REQUIRED

⬭	About 120 metallic grey rocaille beads, 2mm
⯃	4 round steel faceted beads, 4mm
◇	2 round red faceted beads, 4mm
⯃	4 red crystal bicones, 4mm
	1 round black faceted bead, 6mm
	About 1.50m (59in) silver-plated brass wire, 0.25mm
	About 1.50m (59in) black brass wire, 0.25mm

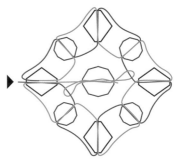

1 Make up two bands of metallic grey rocaille beads each with 28 rows using a 50cm (20in) length of silver-plated wire. Weave a border around them with black wire.

2 Make up a large flower using a 10cm (4in) length of black wire, 4 red bicones and 4 steel faceted beads. Next, attach the round black faceted bead to the flower centre with black wire.

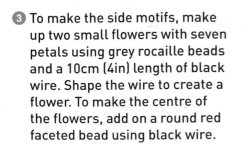

3 To make the side motifs, make up two small flowers with seven petals using grey rocaille beads and a 10cm (4in) length of black wire. Shape the wire to create a flower. To make the centre of the flowers, add on a round red faceted bead using black wire.

4 To assemble your three flowers, take a 15cm (6in) length of black wire and thread it into a bead in one of the two small flowers, leaving a short length of wire. Use the longer end of wire to attach one of the small flowers on to the large flower. Next, thread your wire around the central flower to reach the other side, then attach the other small flower in the same way.

Shown right is the same ring made using white crystal bicones instead of red for the large flower, with a round grey bead at the centre.

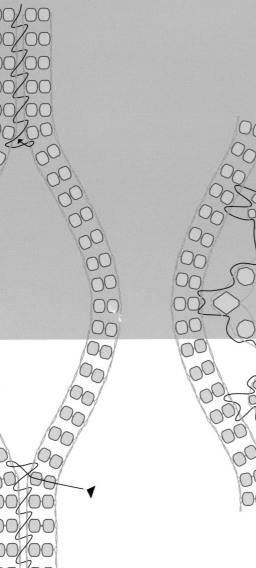

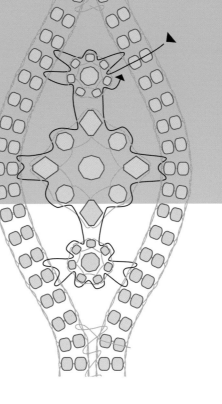

⑤ Join the bands together, leaving the centre 15 rows out of your weaving.

⑥ Position the bouquet of flowers in the centre of your ring, leaving the same amount of space on each side, then attach the motif using a 15cm (6in) length of black wire as shown in the diagram.

You can achieve a very different effect using violet and coral rocaille beads which fit much closer together.

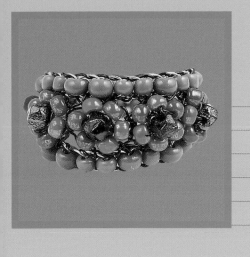

MATERIALS REQUIRED

- 50 mixed grey and violet rocaille beads
- 18 orange rocaille beads
- 4 metallic faceted beads
- 2 round coral resin beads
- About 1m (40in) silver-plated brass wire, 0.25mm
- About 1m (40in) black brass wire, 0.25m

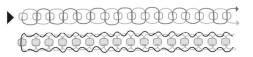

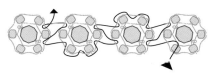

1 Make up two bands of 25 rows using mixed grey and violet rocaille beads and a 50cm (20in) length of silver-plated wire as for the Bouquet ring. Add a border with black wire.

2 Make up four orange flowers with six petals using a 10cm (4in) length of black wire. Finish off your flowers and attach a metallic faceted bead to make their centres.

3 Link the four flowers with a 15cm (6in) length of black wire. Follow the same method as for the Bouquet ring.

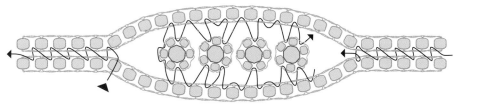

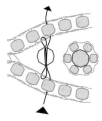

4 Join the two bands using black wire, leaving the centre 15 beads out of your weaving as for the Bouquet. Position the four flowers in the centre of the ring and attach them with black wire as shown in the diagram.

5 Add a coral bead on either side of the four-flower motif by threading a 7cm (3in) length of black wire into one of the edge beads at the point where the bands divide.

SEA URCHIN *

Whether you make it in bronze or silver the 'ball' shape of this original sea urchin ring makes it as comfortable to wear as it is becoming to look at.

MATERIALS REQUIRED

About 46 haematite faceted beads, 4mm

1 antique silver round bead, 12mm

About 30 antique silver rocaille beads, 2.5mm

16 antique silver spacer beads, 6mm

About 80cm (32in) brass wire, 0.25mm

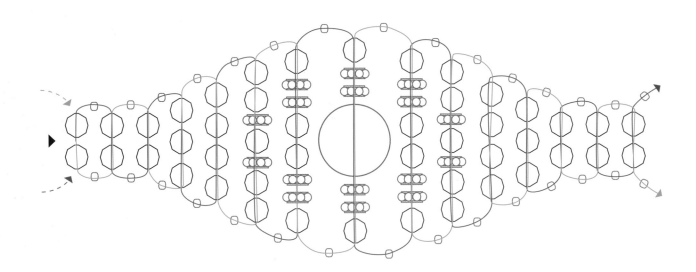

To make the bronze sea urchin, use Jet Nut 2x faceted beads, brass rocaille beads and antique brass spacers.

BUTTERFLY ★★

A large central blue paste bead with chunky bicones make this ring easy to wear and delightfully flashy!

MATERIALS REQUIRED

4 purple crystal bicones, 8mm

1 blue circular paste bead, 8 x 12mm

8 to 10 crystal faceted beads, 4mm

2 gold faceted beads, 3mm

1 tube gold rocaille beads

About 80cm (32in) nylon thread, 0.25mm

2 eyepins, 1 pair round-nosed pliers, 1 pair wire-cutters

① Thread the eyepins into the paste bead support. Trim the pins and bend the ends over, using round-nosed pliers, to form two hoops.

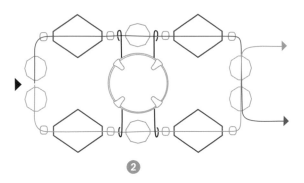

②

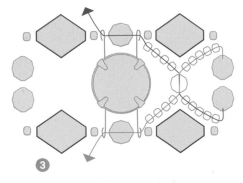

③

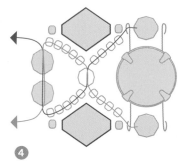

④

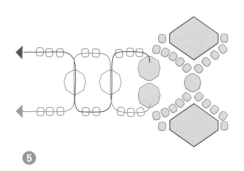

⑤

This variation was made using a red oval paste bead and green 8mm bicones.

SQUARE**

This small square ring is an essential accessory.
Customize it with larger beads or by adding more flower squares.

MATERIALS REQUIRED

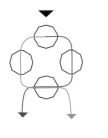

About 25 red faceted beads, 4mm

16 green crystal bicones, 4mm

1 tube gold rocaille beads

About 1.50m (59in) nylon thread, 0.25mm

①   ②   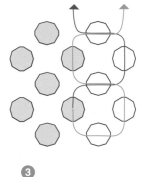 ③   ④

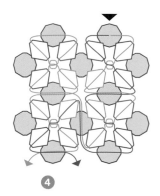

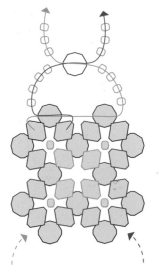 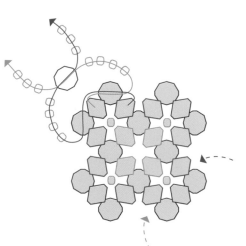

⑤ Attach the band either to the sides of the square (above) or to the corners (right) by threading the nylon around the motif.

Use the base square motif as your starting point to make up 4-square or 6-square rectangular bases to create patchwork-style rings.

DIAMOND ★★★

*Depending on your chosen colour scheme and how you arrange the beads,
you can develop this ring into a carpet of flowers or a highly modern design.*

MATERIALS REQUIRED

About 30 faceted beads, 4mm

28 crystal bicones, 4mm

1 tube rocaille beads

About 1.50m (59in) nylon thread, 0.25mm

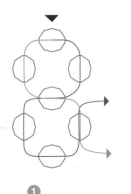

❶

❷

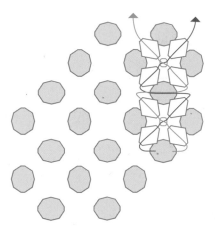

❸ Cover your diamond-shaped base with bicones and rocaille beads as shown in the diagram.

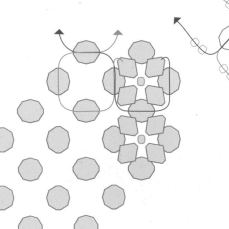

❹ Thread the nylon into your work to get it into the correct position.

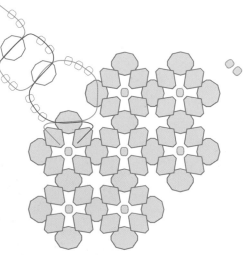

❺ Make up the band.

❻ Attach the finished band to the other side of the motif, then thread each end of nylon around the outside of the motif, adding rocaille beads in the spaces as shown in the diagram.

FINGER GUARD*

An elegant and sophisticated ring, brimming with mystery, that will hug your finger.

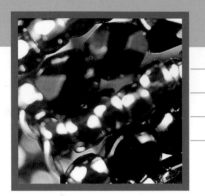

MATERIALS REQUIRED

⬡	22 round faceted beads in metal or black, 2mm
▭ ▭	About 150 translucent brown rocaille beads, 2mm
	About 1.50m (59in) silver-plated brass wire, 0.25mm
	About 50cm (20in) black brass wire, 0.25mm

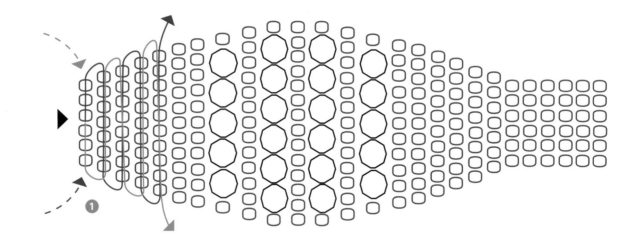

1

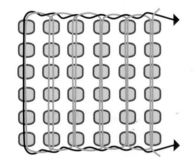

2 To strengthen your ring and to give you neat edges, weave a border with a 50cm (20in) length of black brass wire on each side of the ring.

Alternate grey and violet rocaille beads or brown and transparent beads for variations of this subtle but sophisticated ring.

MIGNONNETTE*

A touch of the retro is added to this contemporary cubist ring which works best using a limited range of colours.

MATERIALS REQUIRED

⬡	About 20 faceted beads, 4mm
▢	3 cube beads, 4mm
◇	4 crystal bicones, 3mm
○	1 tube rocaille beads
	About 1m (40in) nylon thread, 0.25mm

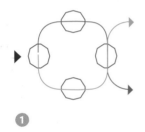

①

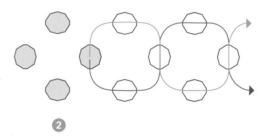

②

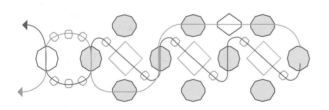

③ Follow the diagram to make the base, then make up the band with the rocaille and the rest of the faceted beads.

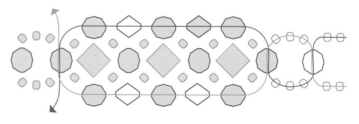

④ Attach the band to the base, then add your bicones.

SIAM*

*A Chinese cloisonné bead and subtle tones give this ring
a delightfully exotic look.*

MATERIALS REQUIRED

	6 round pink glass beads, 6mm
	1 Chinese cloisonné bead, 8 to 12mm
	1 tube gold rocaille beads
	8 to 10 gold faceted beads, 4mm
	About 80cm (32in) nylon thread, 0.25mm
	1 eyepin, 1 pair round-nosed pliers, 1 pair wire-cutters

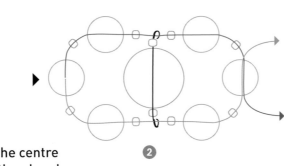 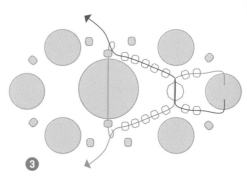

1 Insert the eyepin into the centre cloisonné bead. Trim, then bend the ends of the wire into hoops using round-nosed pliers.

2

3

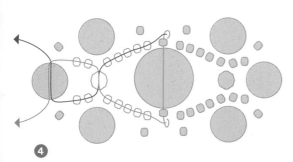

4

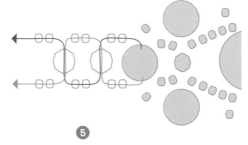

5

To make this variation the cloisonné bead was replaced with a pink paste ball set in gold and surrounded with blue glass beads.

FLOWERING BRANCH ★★★

*Delicate and simple; these flowers, petals and leaves
work well in a variety of ring designs.*

MATERIALS REQUIRED

- About 50 purple rocaille beads, 2mm
- About 20 turquoise rocaille beads, 2mm
- 15 peridot rocaille beads, 2mm
- 15 pink rocaille beads, 2mm
- 1 lemon citrine rocaille bead, 2mm
- About 1.50m (59in) silver-plated brass wire, 0.25mm
- About 1.50m (59in) black brass wire, 0.25mm

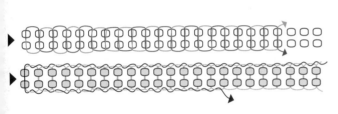

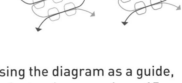

① Make up two bands using a 70cm (28in) length of silver-plated wire and purple rocaille beads as shown in the diagram. Next, make borders for your bands using a 30cm (12in) length of black wire.

② Using the diagram as a guide, make two leaves using a 15cm (6in) length of black wire and pink and peridot rocaille beads.

③ Make a six-petal flower with a 10cm (4in) length of black wire and turquoise rocaille beads. Shape the rows with your fingers to get a flat round motif. Attach a lemon citrine rocaille bead for the centre with a 10cm (4in) length of black wire.

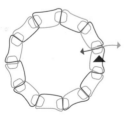

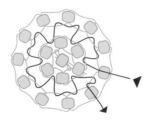

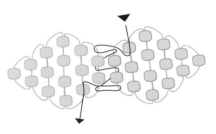

④ Make a round motif using 11 turquoise rocaille beads and a 15cm (6in) length of black wire.

⑤ Place the flower inside the round motif and weave them together with a 15cm (6in) length of black wire.

⑥ Join the two leaves together with a 10cm (4in) length of black wire.

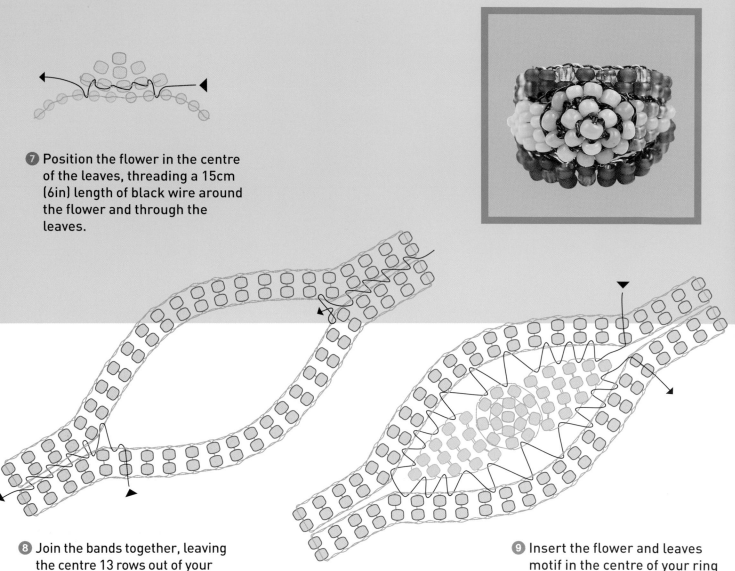

7 Position the flower in the centre of the leaves, threading a 15cm (6in) length of black wire around the flower and through the leaves.

8 Join the bands together, leaving the centre 13 rows out of your weaving.

9 Insert the flower and leaves motif in the centre of your ring and attach it using a 20cm (8in) length of black wire.

To make narrower rings, simply make up one band with two rocaille beads per row to fit your finger. Next, make up the flowers by using the same method as for the Flower Trio or Flowering Branch. Assemble your ring and add a border using black wire as given for the other models in this book.

MATERIALS REQUIRED

- **94 sand-coloured rocaille beads, 2mm**
- **21 pink rocaille beads, 2mm**
- **3 round blue faceted beads, 4mm**
- **About 50cm (20in) silver-plated brass wire, 0.25mm**
- **About 1m (40in) black brass wire, 0.25mm**

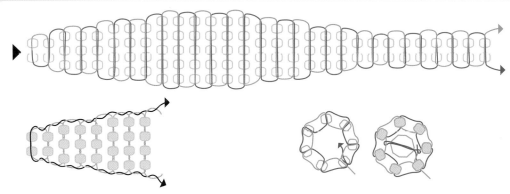

1 Make a ring using sand-coloured rocaille beads and a 50cm (20in) length of silver-plated brass wire.
Next, weave a border for the ring using black wire.

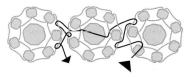

2 Make up three identical flowers with seven petals using pink rocaille beads and attach a blue faceted bead in their centres.

3 Link the three flowers together using a 15cm (6in) length of black brass wire.

4 Attach the flowers to the ring with a 15cm (6in) length of black brass wire, spacing them evenly over the widest part of the ring. Assemble by threading the wire through the ring, following the outline of the motif.

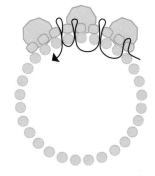

ASTER*

A simple ring that you can customize using your own selection of colours.

MATERIALS REQUIRED

6 faceted seed beads, 7.5 x 5mm

6 crystal bicones, 4mm

1 large round faceted bead, 6mm

6 to 10 round faceted beads, 4mm

1 tube rocaille beads

About 1m (40in) nylon thread, 0.25mm

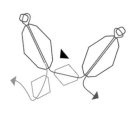

1

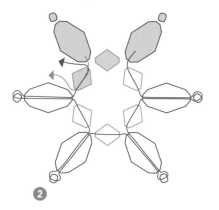

2

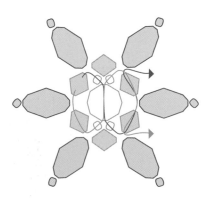

3 Thread one end of the nylon into the nearest bicone, then proceed as shown in the diagrams.

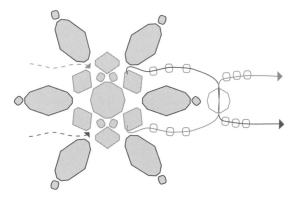

4

BAROQUE ★★

Two rings with clean lines, snug-fitting shapes and bold bead colours.
Make one of each to fit on your middle and your little finger.

TO MAKE THE **LARGE BAROQUE**

18 crystal shadow faceted beads, 3mm

20 crystal shadow faceted beads, 4mm

10 olivine aurora borealis faceted beads, 6mm

1 topaz aurora borealis faceted bead, 10mm

About 42 yellow rocaille beads with metal hole, 2.5mm

8 metal spacer beads in gold, 6mm

2 yellow on gold paste spacer beads, 6mm

About 80cm (32in) brass wire, 0.25mm

TO MAKE THE **SMALL BAROQUE**

36 round green faceted scarab beads, 4mm

4 round green faceted scarab beads, 6mm

1 round green faceted scarab bead, 8mm

32 silver rocaille beads, 2.5mm

2 crystal on silver paste spacer beads, 6mm

4 crystal on silver paste spacer beads, 4mm

About 80cm (32in) brass wire, 0.25mm

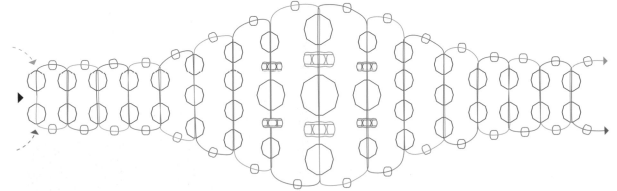

LOTUS*

Simple to make but spectacularly effective,
this sparkling flower is remarkably dazzling.

MATERIALS REQUIRED

34 faceted teardrop beads, 11mm	
1 round or oval perforated metal ring base	
About 1m (40in) nylon thread, 0.25mm	

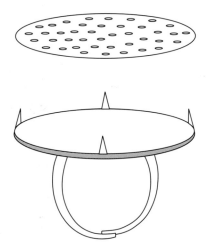

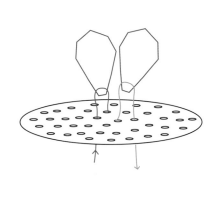

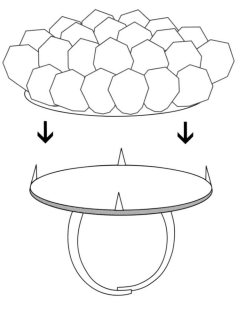

❶ Remove the perforated plate of the ring base.

You could make this ring with smooth teardrop beads on a round or oval support.

❷ Start working at the centre of the plate. Thread the nylon up through one hole and thread on a faceted teardrop bead. Attach it to the plate by going through the next hole. Try to go through all the holes so as to cover the plate and make sure the beads are tightly fixed.

❸ Once you have covered the plate, knot the ends on the underside and thread them back in. Next, attach the plate to the ring base by clipping the claws of the base on to the plate.

LITTLE VIOLETS ★★

*These small and delicate spring flowers are given
a more modern look with brighter colours.*

MATERIALS REQUIRED

⬡	**7 crystal bicones, 6mm**
⬯	**8 crystal bicones, 4mm**
⬡	**6 to 10 round faceted beads, 4mm**
▫	**1 tube rocaille beads**
	About 1m (40in) nylon thread, 0.25mm

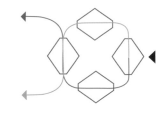

1

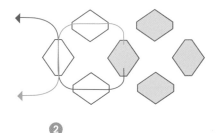

2

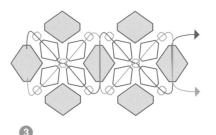

3

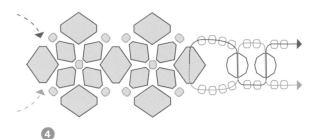

4

SUPPLIERS

This list of suppliers and useful addresses will assist you in sourcing a vast variety of beads, tools and materials for your projects.

UK

The Bead Shop
104–106 Upper Parliament Street,
Nottingham NG1 6LF
tel: 0115 9588899
email: info@mailorder-beads.co.uk
www.mailorder-beads.co.uk

Beadworks
21a Tower Street, Covent Garden,
London WC2H 9NS
tel: 0207 240 0931
www.beadworks.co.uk

Constellation Beads
PO Box 88, Richmond,
North Yorkshire DL10 4FT
tel: 01748 826552
fax: 01748 826552
email: info@constellationbeads.co.uk
www.constellationbeads.co.uk

Creative Beadcraft
20 Beak Street, London W1R 3HA
tel: 0207 6299964
tel (mail order): 01494 778818
email: beads@creativebeadcraft.co.uk
www.creativebeadcraft.co.uk

Gütermann Beads
Perivale-Gütermann Ltd, Bullsbrook
Road, Hayes,
Middlesex UB4 OJR
For nearest stockist tel: 0208 589 1600
UK email: perivale@guetermann.com
Europe email: mail@guetermann.com

Jules Gems
69b Wyle Cop, Bowdler's Passage,
Shrewsbury, Shropshire SY1 1UX
tel: 0845 123 5828 fax: 0845
1235829
email: shop@julesgems.com
www.julesgems.com

Mill Hill Beads
Framecraft Miniatures, Unit 3, Isis
House, Lindon Road, Brownhills, West
Midland WS8 7BW
tel/fax: 01543 360842
tel (international): +44 1543 453154
www.framecraft.co

The Scientific Wire Company
18 Raven Road, London E18 1HW
tel: 0208 505 0002
fax: 0208 5591114
www.wires.co.uk

The Spellbound Bead Company
45 Tamworth Street, Lichfield,
Staffordshire WS13 6JW
tel: 01543 417650
www.spellboundbead.co.uk

Rayher Hobby
Fockestrasse 15, 88471 Laupeim,
Germany
tel: 07392 7005 0
fax: 07392 7005 145
email: info@rayher-hobby.de
www.rayher-hobby.de

USA

Beadbox
1290 N. Scotsdale Road, Tempe
AZ 85281-1703
tel: (480) 967-4080
fax: (480) 967-8555
www.beadbox.com

Beadworks
149 Water Street, Norwalk,
CT 06854
tel: (203) 852-9108
fax: (203) 855-8015
www.beadworks.com

Gütermann of America Inc
8227 Arrowbridge Boulevard,
PO Box 7387,
Charlotte NC 28241-7387
tel: (704) 525-7068
email: info@gutermann-us.com

Mill Hill Beads
For nearest stockist:
Gay Bowles Sales Inc
PO Box 1060, Janesville, WI, 53546
tel: (608) 754-9212
fax: (608) 754-0665
www.millhill.com

USEFUL ADDRESSES

Loisirs et Création
A list of addresses for Loisirs et
Création's twelve outlets can be
obtained by calling +33 1 41 80 64 00

La Droguerie
9–11, rue du Jour
75001 Paris
tel: +33 1 45 08 93 27

Tout à Loisirs
50, rue des Archives
75004 Paris
mail order service available
tel: +33 1 48 87 08 87